GOD'S
STORY
your story

PARTICIPANT'S GUIDE

GOD'S STORY
your story

When His becomes yours

PARTICIPANT'S GUIDE
SIX SESSIONS

MAX LUCADO

WITH KEVIN AND SHERRY HARNEY

ZONDERVAN.com/
AUTHORTRACKER
follow your favorite authors

We want to hear from you. Please send your comments about this book to us in care of zreview@zondervan.com. Thank you.

ZONDERVAN

God's Story, Your Story Participant's Guide
Copyright © 2011 by Max Lucado

Requests for information should be addressed to:
Zondervan, *Grand Rapids, Michigan 49530*

ISBN 978-0-310-88987-8

Published in association with Anvil II Management, Ltd.

Cover design: The A Group
Interior design: Beth Shagene

Printed in the United States of America

11 12 13 14 15 16 /DCI/ 22 21 20 19 18 17 16 15 14 13 12 11 10 9 8 7 6 5 4 3 2

CONTENTS

Of Note

The quotes interspersed through this participant's guide are excerpts from *God's Story, Your Story* by Max Lucado. The book and session introductions have been written by Kevin and Sherry Harney.

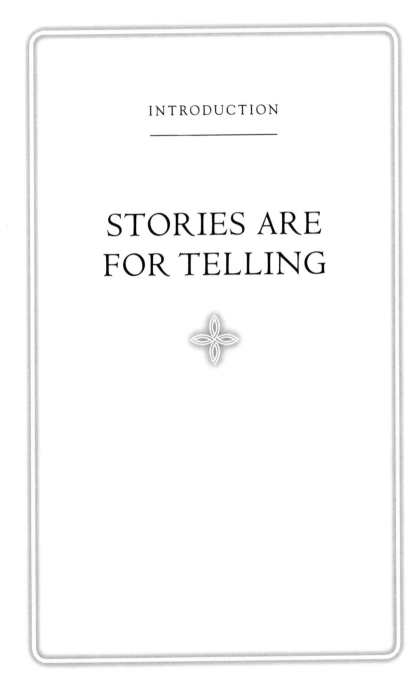

INTRODUCTION

STORIES ARE
FOR TELLING

FROM THE DAWN OF TIME HUMAN BEINGS HAVE LOVED TO TELL stories. In ancient days most stories were kept alive with a rich oral tradition where one generation would pass the stories on to the next through the simple process of telling them ... over and over again.

With time, the stories were written down and captured on paper so that they would be remembered for generations to come. Eventually, with the advent of the printing press, stories could be placed in a book and shared with people all over the world.

Even in our modern time, many of the most influential people in our culture are master storytellers. We call them producers and directors, and they make movies that capture epic themes that touch the heart and stir the imagination.

We love stories ... both hearing and telling them. God has made us this way, because he is the ultimate storyteller. His story precedes the first star being tossed into the darkness of space and will continue after the final breath is taken on this small marble we call earth.

God's story, the story above all other stories, begins in a garden paradise and ends in the glory of heaven. What happens in between is captured in the pages of the Bible. As we listen and hear the story of God's work in human history, we discover that our story is woven into the pages of Scripture. The same God who walked with Adam and Eve wants to walk with us. The God who called the people of Israel to holiness and intimacy with him is speaking to you and me. The Jesus who came to earth to live, die, and rise again is present right where you are gathered with your small group. The story of God is still being written, and we are players in the drama that is unfolding today.

In the six sessions of your small group experience, we invite you to enter into the story. Our hope and prayer is that you will enter this journey of telling your story and hearing the stories of others with great anticipation. This discussion guide is designed to create an environment where group members can tell their story and God can teach and speak through the process.

So share your stories with freedom and joy. And, as you do, you will draw closer to the Master Storyteller in fresh new ways.

WHEN GOD'S STORY BECOMES YOURS

God's story is glorious,
surprising, victorious, and beautiful.
His story, when we really listen closely,
is our story.

INTRODUCTION

Do you remember a time you got lost? Perhaps it was a crowded day at the mall, and you wandered away from Dad and Mom for just a moment, and they were gone. You felt the paralyzing fear of looking around and failing to see the north star of your parents' strong presence. You were lost.

Maybe it was a school trip to the zoo and you inadvertently lingered at the monkey cage while the rest of the class moved on. Before you knew it, you were alone. People were everywhere, but not a face in the crowd was familiar. Lost!

It might have been a drive late at night, and a wrong turn spun you around, and, truth be known, you had no idea where to go next.

These moments of lostness can leave a pit in your stomach and bring fear to your soul ... until the store clerk finds your parents, your teacher taps you on the shoulder and says, "Keep up with the class," or a gas station attendant pulls out a map and shows you how to get back on the interstate.

> *Above and around us God directs a grander saga, written by his hand, orchestrated by his will, unveiled according to his calendar. And you are a part of it.*
>
> —MAX LUCADO

What is even worse is coming to a point in life when we realize that we have lost our way as a human being. We might know our mailing address and how to get to school, work, or church, but we are not sure why we are on this planet. We have no sense of our purpose.

It is in these moments that we look to God, the Master Storyteller, and discover that the best way to understand our story is to listen to his. As we understand God's story and where we fit within it, the haze begins to clear and our story begins to make sense.

TALK ABOUT IT

Tell about a time in your childhood when you got lost and how you felt when you were finally found.

DVD TEACHING NOTES

As you watch the video teaching segment for session 1, featuring Max Lucado, use the following outline to record anything that stands out to you.

An uninformed Munchkin

When everything changes

Getting lost in Grandma's story

What knowing does to us

Knowing God's story

The central message of God's story

Your story indwells God's story

> *Everything changes
> when you know the
> rest of your story.*
> —MAX LUCADO

DVD DISCUSSION

1. Share about a time when someone told you about your family history and certain things about you and your family members began to make sense.

2. Tell about a time you were reading the Bible (God's story) and a light went on in your heart as you realized that this was really your story.

3. If the story of the Bible is going to make sense, it is important to know how it begins and how it ends. In your own words, how does the Bible begin? What are the epic themes that launch us into the story of the Bible (Genesis)?

In your own words, how does the Bible end? What are the epic themes that conclude the story of the Bible (Revelation)?

4. How does your family history help you have a sense of who you are and where your life is going? How does knowing the story of God's family in the Bible help you know who you are and where you are going?

God wants you to know his story. Knowing connects us, links us, bonds us to something greater than we are. Knowing reminds us that we aren't floating on isolated ponds but on a grand river.

—MAX LUCADO

5. Max talked about being dropped into Munchkin Land and being very confused because he did not actually know the storyline of *The Wizard of Oz*. How can reading the Bible without any context or background become a frustrating or dangerous enterprise?

6. What is one of your favorite stories in the Bible and how do you see yourself and your personal story informed by this portion of God's Word?

7. **Read:** John 3:16–17. In the video, Max said that this portion of God's story contains one of the central messages of the Bible. What core messages do you find in this passage?

How can these messages help us understand who we are and how we are to live in this journey through life?

8. **Read:** Ephesians 1:11–14. How do you see God's story and our story woven together in this passage of the Bible?

> *Your story indwells God's. This is the great promise of the Bible.*
> —MAX LUCADO

9. What approach to learning God's Word has most helped you dig in and grow in your love for the Bible?

10. How can your group members pray for you, encourage you, and keep you accountable in reading the Bible and seeking to know God's story in greater depth?

CLOSING PRAYER

Take time as a group to pray in some of the following directions:

- Thank God for his Word, the Bible. Ask him to help you know and love his Word so that you may grow to see your story woven into his story.
- Pray for people you care about who are wandering and lost because they do not know God's story.
- Confess where you have avoided or neglected digging into God's story in the Bible. Pray for

a renewed commitment to read and study the Scriptures with fresh passion.

- Lift up group members who have shared a desire to grow in their knowledge of and love for God's Word. Pray that they will take the steps needed, and exercise the discipline required, to go deep into the truth of the Bible.

> *Your life emerges from the greatest mind and the kindest heart in the history of the universe: the mind and heart of God.*
>
> —MAX LUCADO

BETWEEN SESSIONS

Personal Reflection

Take time to think through three or four of your favorite stories in the Bible. Why are you drawn to these stories? How do you see your story connected to these stories? How did God work in these accounts and what are ways you have seen God work in similar ways in your life?

Personal Action

Contact a patriarch or matriarch in your family and ask if you can spend time with them, face to face or over the phone. Ask questions about your family, their life, and those who have gone before you. Listen with an open heart and seek to discover more about what has formed you and those you love.

Group Engagement

Consider inviting each group member to make a personal commitment to read and reflect on the Bible in the weeks your group meets. Don't have a required reading plan, but have each person set a personal goal. Then, when you meet, ask every person to tell about how they are doing in meeting their own goal and, if possible, to share one lesson they learned in their reading and how it impacts and informs their personal story.

Name: *Personal Goal:*

RECOMMENDED READING

Take time to read chapter 1 of the book *God's Story, Your Story* by Max Lucado.

REFLECTIONS AND NOTES

ORDINARY MATTERS

Our world praises and exalts the "extraordinary";
God meets normal people in the ordinary places of life.

INTRODUCTION

Have you ever seen the motivational posters that grace the walls of so many office buildings? One poster features a crew in a rowboat straining together, the word "TEAMWORK" emblazoned under the photo. Another boasts a stunning ocean shoreline with an enormous rock formation thrusting heavenward from the water. Beneath the picture is the word "INTEGRITY" and the caption, "Do what you know is right ... always. With commitment to your deepest convictions you stand tall against time and tide."

In response to such highly optimistic and cheerful messages, another company, Despair.com, has begun to make its own line of posters. One poster, titled "CONFORMITY," shows a large herd of zebras and the caption, "When people are free to do as they please, they usually imitate each other." Another poster, titled "INDIVIDUALITY," shows beautiful snowflakes floating in the air and text that reads, "Always remember that you are unique. Just like everybody else."

The irony of these two competing companies is that one makes a lot of money selling posters designed

> *God writes his story with people like Joseph and Mary ... and you!*
> —MAX LUCADO

to make people feel special. The other makes a lot of money helping people laugh at that fact that most of us are really quite ordinary and common.

When we read the story of God's people in the Bible we discover that most of them are more like us than we would have guessed. The vast majority of stories in the Bible introduce us to folks that are more ordinary than extraordinary.

TALK ABOUT IT

Who is a person in the Bible (Jesus excluded) whom you find very interesting? What is one way this person seems a lot like you ... normal?

DVD TEACHING NOTES

As you watch the video teaching segment for session 2, featuring Max Lucado, use the following outline to record anything that stands out to you.

A children's Christmas play

God inside a girl

Jesus' birth drips with normalcy

Our everyday life: Norm and Norma

Jesus' connection to the dawn of time

The Word become flesh

Jesus "dwelt" among us

The baby Mary held was connected to the dawn of time. He saw the first ray of sun and heard the first crash of a wave. The baby was born, but the Word never was.

—MAX LUCADO

DVD DISCUSSION

1. In our culture we tend to ignore the normal and ordinary and lift up the unique and extraordinary. Why do you think we do this and why might it be a dangerous way to live?

2. **Read:** Luke 2:1 – 7. God chose Joseph, an ordinary carpenter, to be the stepfather of Jesus, and Mary, a common peasant girl, to be the mother of God incarnate. As this Jewish couple came to Bethlehem for the census, what would people have seen by looking at them? How might people have responded if Joseph tried to tell them who Mary was and the true identity of the baby in her womb?

The story of Jesus' birth drips with normalcy. Normal has calluses like Joseph, stretch marks like Mary. Normal stays up late with laundry and wakes up early for work. Normal drives carpool wearing a bathrobe and slippers. Normal is Norm and Norma, not Prince and Princess.

—MAX LUCADO

3. In the video Max said, "The Christmas hope is that God indwells the everydayness of our world." What is one way you experience the presence and hope of God as you walk through a normal day?

4. God uses normal people such as Mary and Joseph to accomplish his will in this world. What is one way God has worked through your normal life in a way that is surprising and exciting for you?

5. If we are not careful, even in the church we can make people feel ordinary and unimportant. How can we make

the people in our church feel loved and welcomed? What can we do to reach out to those who are visiting our church for the first time to ensure that they feel embraced and wanted?

6. **Read:** John 1:1 – 3; Genesis 1:1 – 2; and Colossians 1:15 – 16. What do you learn about Jesus in these passages? In light of who Jesus really is, why is his humble birth so surprising and shocking?

The Word of God entered the world with the cry of a baby. Jesus, the Maker of the universe, the one who invented time and created breath, was born into a family too humble to swing a bed for a pregnant mom-to-be.

—MAX LUCADO

7. In the video, Max made this provocative statement, "The splendor of the first Christmas is the lack thereof." What do you think he is getting at?

8. Jesus came as one of us; he pitched his tent in an ordinary neighborhood. How can we be the presence of Jesus right where God has placed us?

9. Tell about an ordinary person that God used to write his story in your life. How is your life richer because of this person?

10. Consider someone God has placed in your life whom you might influence for him. How does God want to use you

to help write his story in their life? How can your group members encourage you and cheer you on in your effort?

CLOSING PRAYER

Take time as a group to pray in some of the following directions:

- Thank God that he came among us not as royalty, but as a normal person.

- Ask God to help you enter your neighborhood, workplace, social settings, wherever, as an ordinary person carrying the extraordinary love of Jesus.

- Pray for your church to have a welcoming heart that embraces common people. Pray against any spirit of elitism that might creep into your church.

- Pray for the presence of God's Holy Spirit to be so welcome in your heart and home that other people actually notice something different about you.

> *God became an embryo and indwelt the belly of a village girl. Christ in Mary. God in Christ.*
>
> —MAX LUCADO

BETWEEN SESSIONS

Personal Reflection

Think about how you can notice the presence of God in the flow of your normal day. Also, reflect on ways you can bring the presence of God in organic and natural ways into every part of your day. Invite Jesus to shine in and through you so that others will see his presence and want to know him.

Personal Action

Examine your heart. If you are guilty of adopting attitudes or actions that set you above and apart from others with a spirit of elitism, confess this to God and pray for a new attitude of humility and love for others.

Group Engagement

Consider having your group members commit to make a point of greeting one new person every Sunday for the coming month. If you don't see anyone new, be sure to welcome a person you don't know very well. Seek to make people feel welcomed and embraced.

RECOMMENDED READING

Take time to read chapter 4 of *God's Story, Your Story* by Max Lucado.

REFLECTIONS AND NOTES

YOU HEAR A VOICE YOU CAN TRUST

In a world of voices crying
for our attention,
there is one that we must learn
to hear with crystal clarity.

INTRODUCTION

In 1971 the Canadian rock group, Five Man Electrical Band, wrote a song that hit number three on the U.S. *Billboard* "Hot 100" and sold over a million copies. You might remember "Signs"—especially the catchy refrain:

> *Sign, sign, everywhere a sign*
> *Blocking out the scenery, breaking my mind*
> *Do this, don't do that, can't you read the sign?*

Throughout the song, a man expresses his frustration with all the signs (voices) telling him what to do or not to do. One voice says that he can't get a job at a local business if he is one of those "long-haired freaky people." Another lets him know he will be shot if he trespasses on private property. Still another informs him that the way he dresses and the fact that he does not have a membership card prohibits his inclusion in a private club.

In the final verse, he sees a sign on a church that says, "Everybody welcome, come in, kneel down, and pray," and he goes inside. When the offering plate comes by, he has no money so he writes his own little sign, his personal message to God: "Thank you, Lord, for thinking about me; I'm alive and doing fine."

All through time human beings have faced the challenge of learning to hear and recognize the voice of the one true God through the clutter of culture, societal messages, competing religious traditions, and the general noise of life's traffic. Many signs, messages, and voices seem to battle for our attention. If we are not careful, we can listen to the wrong voice, follow the wrong sign, and end up headed down a wrong road or even driving off a cliff.

Some believe that Jesus masterminded the greatest scheme in the history of humanity, that he out-Ponzied the swindlers and outhustled the hucksters. If that were true, billions of humans have been fleeced into following a first-century pied piper over the edge of a cliff.

—MAX LUCADO

TALK ABOUT IT

What are some of the big messages being declared in culture today and what are some possible consequences if we embrace and follow them?

DVD TEACHING NOTES

As you watch the video teaching segment for session 3, featuring Max Lucado, use the following outline to record anything that stands out to you.

Flying blind

Many voices

Jesus' important question

Peter's reply

Jesus' claims about himself

Jesus' impact on others

Wonderful truth about Jesus

DVD DISCUSSION

1. What are some ways Jesus comes alongside of us during our dark times to give direction and hope when we can't see what lies ahead?

2. Describe a person who has functioned as a wise, godly voice speaking into your life in both good and hard times. How has God used this person to give direction and provide safety on your journey?

3. When Jim O'Neill realized he was flying blind, he sent out a Mayday distress call. Tell about a time you cried out to God with a Mayday prayer and how he answered and came to your side.

4. What is an area of your life, right now, where you feel like you are flying blind? How can your group members pray for you and fly at your side during this challenging time?

5. What competing voices in your life are calling for your attention and distracting you from hearing the voice of Jesus? What can you do to minimize the volume of these voices to better hear the voice of Jesus?

6. **Read:** Mark 8:27 – 30. People in Jesus' day had all kinds of theories about who Jesus was. What were some of these theories and how would the people have been impacted if they believed these inaccurate voices?

Had Jesus been a fraud or trickster, the first Christian congregation would have died a stillborn death. People would have denounced the miracles of Christ. But they did just the opposite. They believed in them . . . and him!

—MAX LUCADO

7. Peter was the only disciple to give a clear and confident declaration of who Jesus was (and for the record ... he was right!). Tell about a time in your life when the reality that Jesus is Messiah, Savior, and Lord became very real and personal for you. How did this awareness impact your ability to hear and follow the voice of Jesus?

8. **Read:** Matthew 9:4–7; 11:11; 12:6–8; 28:18–19; John 4:12–14; and 14:13–14. Some people like to say, "Jesus was a decent fellow, a great teacher, a wonderful moral person, but nothing more." In light of these passages, what do we learn about Jesus that shows he was far more than just a good person?

9. One of the ways we can see the truth of a person's message is the fruit that it bears. What are some of the ways the world has been made a better place because of the life and teaching of Jesus carried on by his followers? What are one or two ways your life has been made better because you have a relationship with Jesus?

> *Jesus transformed common dockworkers and net casters into the authors of history's greatest book and founders of its greatest movement.*
>
> —MAX LUCADO

10. Jesus is exactly who Peter declared him to be — the Savior who is with us at all times. What practical steps can you take to stay connected with Jesus throughout your day? How can you listen for his voice in dark times as well as times when things are going great?

CLOSING PRAYER

Take time as a group to pray in some of the following directions:

- Pray for ears to hear the loving, clear voice of Jesus speaking through the Word and by the Holy Spirit as you walk through your days.

- Ask God to give you and your group members discerning hearts and attentive ears to identify the false voices that speak in our world and wisdom to reject the messages that are contrary to God's Word and truth.

- Confess where you have been drawn into listening to unhealthy voices and ask God to help you shut off the source of false messages.

- Thank God for speaking through his Word, both written and incarnate.

What if Jesus really was, and is, the Son of God? If so, then we can relish this wonderful truth: we never travel alone. We do not know what the future holds. But we are not alone.

—MAX LUCADO

BETWEEN SESSIONS

Personal Reflection

Many voices cry out for our attention. Make a list of some of the unhealthy voices and sources of information that flow into your life:

Now make a list of the sources of healthy and Christ-honoring information that can impact your life:

Think and pray about practical ways you can turn down the volume of the unhealthy voices and increase your openness to the positive sources.

Personal Action

With the flood of voices screaming in our hearts and grabbing for our attention, it is always safe to listen to Jesus. During the coming month read the Gospels (Matthew, Mark, Luke, and John). Pay special attention to the words and teachings of Jesus. Let these become the filter you use to determine what other voices are worth hearing.

Group Engagement

One way to increase our learning and open our ears more to the voice of Jesus is sharing what we are learning from our personal study of God's Word. We can never go wrong when we read the Bible and listen for the voice of the Holy Spirit. Commit to share via email one or two things God is teaching you in his Word each week for the coming month. This way, you will all learn from each other and increase your ability to hear the truth of God.

RECOMMENDED READING

Take time to read chapter 5 of *God's Story, Your Story* by Max Lucado.

REFLECTIONS AND NOTES

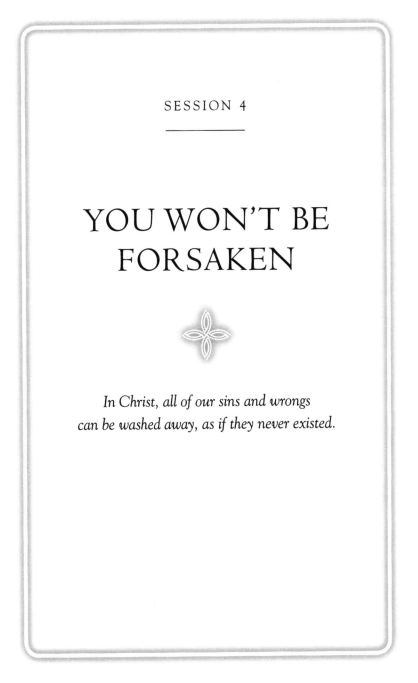

YOU WON'T BE FORSAKEN

*In Christ, all of our sins and wrongs
can be washed away, as if they never existed.*

INTRODUCTION

Where in the world do we get the idea that we have to work to prove we are worthy? At what point in our existence do we start feeling judged, graded, and measured on how we perform? What makes us feel like we must make restitution for our wrongs or we will never be acceptable?

Sadly, the tests and measurements begin with our first breath and cry as we leave the womb. A doctor or nurse plops us on a scale and weighs us like a trout fresh out of water. We are measured for length and our skin tone is assessed. Every baby is given an APGAR score within minutes of birth. Of course, this is not an official competition, but the measurements do matter to parents.

We praise, celebrate, and measure almost everything: the age a child rolls over, uses a potty chair, walks, talks, reads, and rides a bike. We give stars on charts in Sunday school for attendance, Bible memory verses, and bringing a Bible to church. As soon as a child can toddle we put them in cute little cleats and usher them onto a sports field and teach them how to win. As soon as school starts, children get checks and minuses and, later, years of report cards. When we enter the world of employment, yearly evaluations and raises (or no raises) tell us what our boss thinks we are worth.

Where do we get this strange notion that we must perform, work for what we have, and measure up? The answer is quite simple: it is drilled into our emotional DNA every day of our life. Do poorly ... pay the price! Behave well ... get praised! Drop the ball ... lose your spot on first string. Get good grades ... promises of scholarships come in the mail.

Into our orderly and consistent program of cause and effect steps Jesus. But he does not play by our rules. He disrupts the whole system. Jesus turns it all upside down and inside out. And when we get to know how Jesus does things ... a new life begins.

> *Jesus' sacrifice is a sufficient one. Our merits don't enhance it. Our stumbles don't diminish it. The sacrifice of Christ is a total and unceasing and accomplished work.*
>
> –MAX LUCADO

TALK ABOUT IT

Tell about a moment that occurred as you were growing up when you realized so much of life is based on how you perform and how hard you work.

DVD TEACHING NOTES

As you watch the video teaching segment for session 4, featuring Max Lucado, use the following outline to record anything that stands out to you.

The vest system

Our attempts to work ourselves out of our vests

Focus of the cross

Jesus forsaken

Christ dressed in our vests

Christ's sufficient sacrifice: the removal of our vests

Our new wardrobe

God does not simply remove our failures; he dresses us in the goodness of Christ! "For all of you who were baptized into Christ have clothed yourselves with Christ" (Galatians 3:27).

—MAX LUCADO

DVD DISCUSSION

1. Often we try to remove our vests of past shame and poor choices by doing good works. What are some of the ways we try to "work off" our vests and what are some problems with this approach?

2. Max pointed out that the Bible does not tell stories about how to work off our vests of shame. Rather, it offers accounts of how God's story redeems our story. What is a Bible passage or story that you like because it paints a picture of God's redemption and love for us, in spite of our sin and brokenness?

3. Without using names or details, tell about a time when someone confessed to you that they were wearing a vest of sin and shame. What counsel did you give them after they acknowledged their struggle?

4. If you are still wearing a vest of sin and shame, share its nature (if you're comfortable doing so) and why you have a hard time taking it off and giving it to Jesus. How can your group members pray for you as you seek to remove this vest?

5. **Read:** Matthew 27:32 – 56. According to the Gospels and the rest of the Bible, what did Jesus do to remove our vests and set us free from shame? What did the Father do in this process of offering us cleansing and freedom?

> *Jesus' death on the cross is not a secondary theme in Scripture; it is the core.*
>
> —MAX LUCADO

6. **Read:** 2 Corinthians 5:21; Isaiah 53:3 – 7; Galatians 3:13; and Romans 5:6 – 8. How did Jesus take our sins (vests of shame) on himself? How does this affect the way God sees us and the way we should see ourselves?

7. Though disputed by some, the story of Flight 255 is a compelling picture of a mother apparently wrapping herself around her daughter to take the impact of the fall and save her daughter's life. How does this story capture the love and grace of Jesus and what he did for us on the cross?

8. Picture Jesus on the cross and all of your sins (vests) and the judgment for them being placed on him. What would you say to Jesus if he were here right now and you could thank him for taking all your sin and shame on himself as he suffered and died on the cross?

> *When you make God's story yours, he covers you in Christ.*
> —MAX LUCADO

9. **Read:** 1 Peter 2:24 and 2 Corinthians 5:21. In the video, Max talked about the "Great Exchange" that happened on the cross. Our sins became Christ's and he bore them. His righteousness has become ours and we wear it like a beautiful new vest. How have you experienced the righteousness of Christ transforming your heart and life since becoming a follower of Jesus?

10. **Read:** 1 Peter 2:9 – 10; 2 Corinthians 6:1; 1 Corinthians 3:16 – 17; and Ephesians 2:10. When we receive Jesus and let him remove our vests of sin and shame, he gives us a new identity. Who do we become when we follow Jesus and let him give us a new life and future? How does our knowledge of our new identity send us into a whole new future?

CLOSING PRAYER

Take time as a group to pray in some of the following directions:

- Thank the Father for sending his own Son to die in your place and for your sins. Give praise to the Holy Spirit for drawing you to the heart of Jesus. Thank Jesus for paying the price to remove your vests, be cleansed of sin, and walk in freedom.

- Thank God for clothing you in his righteousness and pray for power to walk in this new life he offers.

- Ask God to give you boldness and clarity of mind as you seek to share the story of his grace and Jesus' sacrifice with family and friends who have not yet received this gift.

- Confess where you are still wearing vests of shame and ask for courage to place them at the foot of the cross.

Headline this truth: When God sees you, he sees his Son, not your sin. God "blots out your transgressions" and "remembers your sins no more" (Isaiah 43:25). No probation. No exception. No reversals.

—MAX LUCADO

BETWEEN SESSIONS

Personal Reflection

Read: Matthew 28:16–20 and 1 Peter 3:15. We are called to share the story of Jesus and give witness to what God has done in us. What might you say to *one* of these people if they were open to hear about your relationship with Jesus:

- A Christian friend who keeps putting on the same old vest of shame and guilt

- A non-Christian friend who does not believe God wants to forgive his past and give him a new future

- A teenager who grew up in the church but has never really understood God's love and grace

- A grade-school girl who wonders if there is a God out there who cares about her

Personal Action

Make a list of any vests you seem to keep taking back and wanting to wear again. Ask God for such a deep understanding of the sacrifice of Jesus that you will never wear these again.

Group Engagement

Over the coming month, be sure to ask a number of your group members these two questions:

> Are you making sure you never wear your old vests of shame over past sin?

> Are you proudly wearing the garments Jesus has placed on you?

RECOMMENDED READING

Take time to read chapter 6 of *God's Story, Your Story* by Max Lucado.

REFLECTIONS AND NOTES

YOUR FINAL CHAPTER BECOMES A PREFACE

In life, the end is often exactly that, the end.
With Jesus, the end can become the beginning.

INTRODUCTION

Most of us have attended a funeral or stood at the graveside of a person we truly loved. Moments like these are sobering, with a sense of finality that we tend to avoid in our day-to-day life. We face a spectrum of emotions that are deep and hard to put into words.

One moment we are thinking about how we will miss them. Our mind wanders to all they meant to us and how our life will be different without them ... tears flow.

The next moment we are talking with someone about how precious this person was to us and we recount a moment of intense joy and delight that we shared with them ... we smile and even laugh.

Five minutes later our mind wanders forward to the coming year as we seek to imagine Christmas, a birthday, or Valentine's Day without them ... and our heart grows heavy.

Up and down we go, like a child on a teeter-totter. Joy and sorrow. Tears and laughter. Highs and lows. This is the journey we travel when a loved one dies. Even Jesus wept at the tomb of Lazarus (John 11:35).

But covering the whole experience is a profound certainty and awareness that, if our loved ones were Christians, we will see them again. This is not the end of the story. God has already won. Death can't hold them. Jesus is on the throne … risen and glorious. The grave is not their final destination; heaven is their home … and ours as well.

The bodily resurrection means everything. If Jesus lives on only in spirit and deeds, he is but one of a thousand dead heroes. But if he lives on in flesh and bone, he is the King who pressed his heel against the head of death.

—MAX LUCADO

TALK ABOUT IT

Tell about a time that a Christian family member or friend passed away. What feelings did you have during this season of loss and how did you experience both sorrow and joy?

DVD TEACHING NOTES

As you watch the video teaching segment for session 5, featuring Max Lucado, use the following outline to record anything that stands out to you.

The folly of not having an exit strategy

No dream of a Sunday morning miracle

Plans to embalm Jesus, not talk to him

Cadaver turned King: he is risen!

The bodily resurrection of Jesus means everything

Promise about our grave

Death is not the final chapter

"He has risen." Three words in English. Just one in Greek. Egerthe. So much rests on the validity of this one word. If it is false, then the whole of Christianity collapses like a poorly told joke. Yet, if it is true, then God's story has turned your final chapter into a preface.

—MAX LUCADO

DVD DISCUSSION

1. We live in a day and age when many people don't look farther down the road than *today* or maybe *this weekend*. Carl McCunn's journal included these fateful words: "I think I should have used more foresight about arranging my departure." Why do so many people walk through this life failing to plan for their ultimate departure? What do Christians have to share with others that will help them get ready for the end of life on this planet?

2. Satan would love to keep every man, woman, and child so distracted and busy that they never face their own mortality and the reality that death looms in front of us all. What are some of the Enemy's distractions that keep people from asking important spiritual and eternal questions?

3. If a non-Christian friend or family member asked you, "What do you believe will happen to you when this life ends?" how would you explain eternity and your faith and confidence in God in a way that would make sense to them?

4. If a nonbelieving family member or friend was drawing near the end of their life and they asked you, "How can I prepare for eternity and be ready to meet God?" what would you say to them? How would you help them prepare?

> *What Jesus did with his own grave,*
> *he promises to do with yours: empty it.*
> —MAX LUCADO

5. **Read:** Luke 18:31–33; 24:45–47. Imagine you were one of the disciples who walked with Jesus and heard him talk about his death and resurrection with such crystal clarity. How could they have heard these words and still not have realized that Jesus was actually going to rise from the dead? Give examples of ways that we hear Jesus declare things with clarity and conviction but still don't fully embrace the truth of what he says.

6. In the video Max talked about how the disciples got stuck on Saturday (Jesus' body in the tomb), but they needed to move into Sunday (Christ risen and alive!). How can Christians today get stuck on Saturday and forget that we live in the glorious victory of Resurrection Sunday? What can we do to inspire ourselves, and others, to live in the hope and reality of Easter Sunday?

7. **Read:** 1 Corinthians 15:12 – 18. Why is absolute confidence in the bodily resurrection of Jesus so critical to the Christian faith? According to the apostle Paul, what are the implications for us if Christ has not risen from the dead?

Jesus has risen. Not risen from sleep. Not risen from confusion. Not risen from stupor or slumber. Not spiritually raised from the dead; physically raised. The women and disciples didn't see a phantom or experience a sentiment. They saw Jesus in the flesh.

—MAX LUCADO

8. **Read:** 1 Corinthians 15:42 – 58. How does the resurrection of Jesus and our assurance of eternal life, through faith in his name, impact our lives today and forever?

9. **Read:** John 11:17 – 27. How does Jesus connect his resurrection and the eternal condition of those who have faith

in him? If we believe these words of Jesus, how should our assurance of eternal life impact the way we live today?

10. When we are assured of Jesus' resurrection and confident that heaven is our home, everything changes. What transformation have you experienced in *one* of these areas as you have grown more and more confident that the final chapter of your life is really just a preface to eternity with God?

- How you view this life and the way you invest your time ...

- How you share God's love and message of grace with others ...

- How you use your resources and the way you view material things ...

- How you view and treat people who have not yet entered a saving relationship with Jesus ...

- Some other area of your life ...

Which one of these areas would you desire to grow in and how can your small group members pray for you as you journey forward?

CLOSING PRAYER

Take time as a group to pray in some of the following directions:

* Thank Jesus for his sacrificial death in your place on the cross ... to deal with all your sins. And thank him for his glorious resurrection and the certainty you have that heaven will be your home because he has opened and prepared the way!

* Pray for people you love and care about who have still not embraced God's plan for their life and eternity.

* Confess where you get stuck on Saturday and forget to celebrate the joy and confidence that result in knowing that Sunday has come and Jesus has risen.

* Ask God to help you walk in the resurrection power of Jesus each and every day of your life.

> *Death is not the final chapter in your story. In death you will step into the arms of the One who declared, "I am the resurrection and the life. He who believes in me will live, even though he dies; and whoever lives and believes in me will never die" (John 11:25–26).*
>
> —MAX LUCADO

BETWEEN SESSIONS

Personal Reflection

Read: 1 Corinthians 15. Reflect on the importance of Jesus' resurrection — to you personally and on a broader level. What would be different if Jesus had not risen? How has hope invaded our world through the resurrection? What do you have to look forward to because Jesus rose from the dead and you have received his grace?

Personal Action

So many people have no "exit strategy" from this world. They are caught up in the distractions and stuff of life and don't think past the next week or month. Commit to pray for family and friends who have not entered a life-saving friendship with Jesus. Ask God to give you opportunities to move from prayer into action as you share with others what the resurrection of Jesus means to you and what it could mean in their life ... and eternity.

Group Engagement

Most communities are home to service and mission organizations that serve meals (or provide other assistance) to the poor. Find a date (either a holiday or maybe a weekend in the near future) where your group could serve together in a local ministry. If you have kids, you might want to invite them to take part. As you prepare to serve and as you engage with people in this time of need, pray for opportunities to share not only your time, food, and service, but also the hope of the resurrected Jesus.

RECOMMENDED READING

Take time to read the conclusion of *God's Story, Your Story* by Max Lucado.

REFLECTIONS AND NOTES

YOU WILL FINALLY GRADUATE

We cling tightly to this life,
but for followers of Jesus,
the best is yet to come!

INTRODUCTION

Promises, promises, promises! Advertisers constantly pummel us with pitches that guarantee all sorts of things. Drive this car and your life will shift into a new gear of excitement and meaning. Wear this deodorant and the ladies will flock to you with irresistible passion. Use this weight-loss program and the pounds will melt off in a matter of weeks (and apparently your teeth will become whiter, you'll smile more, and you'll get a new hair style too).

Unfortunately, promises, promises, and more promises often lead to cynicism and skepticism.

The new car does not bring the excitement we expected, but only higher insurance premiums. The deodorant does not make us a magnet for the affection we desire ... it only makes us smell like we are trying a little too hard. The newest weight-loss fad really helps for the first week, and then we look in the mirror to discover that our hips, teeth, and hair look pretty much the same as they did when we started the program.

With the hype of too many promises that fail to deliver, we can become numb to any new promise we hear ... even promises from God. In particular, when we receive assurances of a better world beyond this one, eternal hope, a heavenly home that awaits us, and the promise of a glorious new body, it can all seem too good to be true.

If we are not careful, we can become jaded and cynical ... even when it comes to God's promise of heaven.

> *Heaven has scheduled a graduation. Sin will no longer be at war with our flesh. Eyes won't lust, thoughts won't wander, hands won't steal, our minds won't judge, appetites won't rage, and our tongues won't lie. We will be brand-new.*
>
> —MAX LUCADO

TALK ABOUT IT

Tell about a time you tried a new product with high hopes and expectations only to end up discouraged and disheartened when the advertising promises did not match your reality.

DVD TEACHING NOTES

As you watch the video teaching segment for session 6, featuring Max Lucado, use the following outline to record anything that stands out to you.

Graduation is no small matter

All things in Christ

Sigh of sadness in suffering

Jesus heals

We shall be like Jesus

No more curse

How to live these days on earth

DVD DISCUSSION

1. In the video, Max talked about how the same night became the graduation date of his daughter (from school) and his mother (from this life). How is the day a Christian dies really a graduation day? What are we graduating from and what are we graduating to?

2. **Read:** 1 Corinthians 15:35 – 44. One promise God makes is that when this life ends, we will receive a new and eternal body. How will our new bodies be an upgrade compared to the ones we have right now? What is one thing that excites you about receiving a new body?

3. **Read:** Mark 7:31 – 35. Jesus did a lot of healing while he was on this earth. As you look at this account and others recorded in the four Gospels (Matthew, Mark, Luke, and John), what do you learn about how Jesus healed? What do you learn about why Jesus healed people?

> *I hate disease.*
> *I'm sick of it.*
> *So is Christ.*
> —MAX LUCADO

4. We know that when this life ends and we graduate, we will receive new bodies. Until then, the Bible tells us that we can and should pray for healing for those who are sick and face physical struggles (James 5:13 – 16). Who are you praying for right now and how can your group members join you in both praying for and caring for these people?

5. **Read:** 1 John 3:1 – 3. What do you learn about God in this passage? What do you learn about yourself?

6. First John 3:2 assures us that one day (postgraduation) "we shall be like [Jesus]." In what ways are we already becoming more like Jesus? In what ways will we be even more like Jesus after our final graduation day? In what ways will Jesus always be unique and different from us?

7. **Read:** Romans 7:15 – 19. The apostle Paul is brutally honest about the struggle we all face with sin in this life. What does Paul say about our battle with sin and how do his words resonate with your experience?

8. In light of what the apostle Paul teaches in Romans 7, what is one thing you really want to do, but find it difficult to follow through on?

What is one thing you find yourself doing, but you hate it and want to stop? How can your group pray for you and keep you accountable in these areas of your life?

9. **Read:** Revelation 22:1 – 3. After our graduation day, the curse of sin will be gone. How does this promise give hope in this life? What are some sins and struggles that you look forward to dismissing?

10. **Read:** 2 Corinthians 4:16 – 18 and Romans 8:18. How does the apostle Paul compare this life to the life to come? How can a passage like this help us when we face pain, struggles, and loss?

Why is meditating on heaven and remembering what comes after graduation day so important for Christians?

CLOSING PRAYER

Take time as a group to pray in some of the following directions:

- Thank God that heaven really is your home and that Jesus has already gone ahead of you to prepare the way.

- Tell God of your heartache concerning the pain and struggles of this world. Pray for his compassion to fill your heart so that you can help bring his grace, love, and comfort to those who are hurting.

- Lift up people you care about who are facing physical ailments and challenges. Ask for the grace of God, his comfort, and his healing touch to be upon them.

- Thank God for the people you love who have gone before you to heaven. Praise God that they were part of your life for a season and that they are with Jesus now.

> *Some of you indwell such road-weary bodies: knees ache, eyes dim, skin sags. Others exited the womb on an uphill ride. While I have no easy answers for your struggle, I implore you to see your challenge in the scope of God's story. View these days on earth as but the opening lines of his sweeping saga.*
>
> —MAX LUCADO

IN THE COMING DAYS

Personal Reflection

One day the curse of sin will be gone (Revelation 22:3), but until our final graduation we will do battle with it. This week identify two or three areas of temptation with which the Enemy tries to lure you. Then do three things: (1) pray for eyes to see and power to overcome the tactics of the Enemy; (2) take practical steps to avoid places and situations that would open the door to possible temptation in these areas of struggle; (3) invite a trusted member of your small group to pray for you and keep you accountable to walk in holiness in these areas.

Personal Action

Make a list of people you care about who are dealing with physical ailments and ongoing health issues. Commit to pray for them on a weekly basis. As circumstances permit, give them an occasional call and pray with them over the phone, or meet with them for prayer. When God answers prayers for healing, praise him and give him the glory. When there is no healing, continue praying and place your trust in God's sovereign power and wisdom.

Group Engagement

As you wrap up this study, consider a next step you can take as a group. If you have not studied *The Story* together, talk about doing the thirty-one-week *Story Adult Curriculum* small group study.

RECOMMENDED READING

Take time to read all of *God's Story, Your Story* by Max Lucado.

REFLECTIONS AND NOTES

SMALL GROUP
LEADER HELPS

To ensure a successful small group experience, read the following information before beginning.

GROUP PREPARATION

Whether your small group has been meeting together for years or is gathering for the first time, be sure to designate a consistent time and place to work through the six sessions. Once you establish the when and where of your times together, select a facilitator who will keep discussions on track and an eye on the clock. If you choose to rotate this responsibility, assign the six sessions to their respective facilitators upfront, so that group members can prepare their thoughts and questions prior to the session they are responsible for leading. Follow the same assignment procedure should your group want to serve any snacks/beverages.

A NOTE TO FACILITATORS

As facilitator, you are responsible for honoring the agreed-upon timeframe of each meeting, for prompting helpful discussion among your group, and for keeping the dialogue equitable by drawing out quieter members and helping more talkative members to remember that others' insights are valued in your group.

You might find it helpful to preview each session's video teaching segment and then scan the "DVD Discussion" questions that pertain to it, highlighting various questions that you want to be sure to cover during your group's meeting. Ask God in advance of your time together to guide your group's discussion, and then be sensitive to the direction he wishes to lead.

Urge participants to bring their participant's guide, pen, and a Bible to every gathering. Encourage them to consider buying a copy of the *God's Story, Your Story* book by Max Lucado to supplement this study.

SESSION FORMAT

Each session of the participant's guide includes the following group components:

- **"Introduction"** — an entrée to the session's topic, which may be read by a volunteer or summarized by the facilitator
- **"Talk About It"** — an icebreaker question that relates to the session topic and invites input from every group member
- **"DVD Teaching Notes"** — an outline of the session's 10 – 12 minute video teaching for group members to follow along and take notes if they wish
- **"DVD Discussion"** — video-related and Bible exploration questions that reinforce the session content and elicit personal input from every group member
- **"Closing Prayer"** — several prayer cues to guide group members in closing prayer

Additionally, in each session you will find a **"Between Sessions"** section that includes suggestions for personal and group response, recommended reading from the *God's Story, Your Story* book, and a journal page.